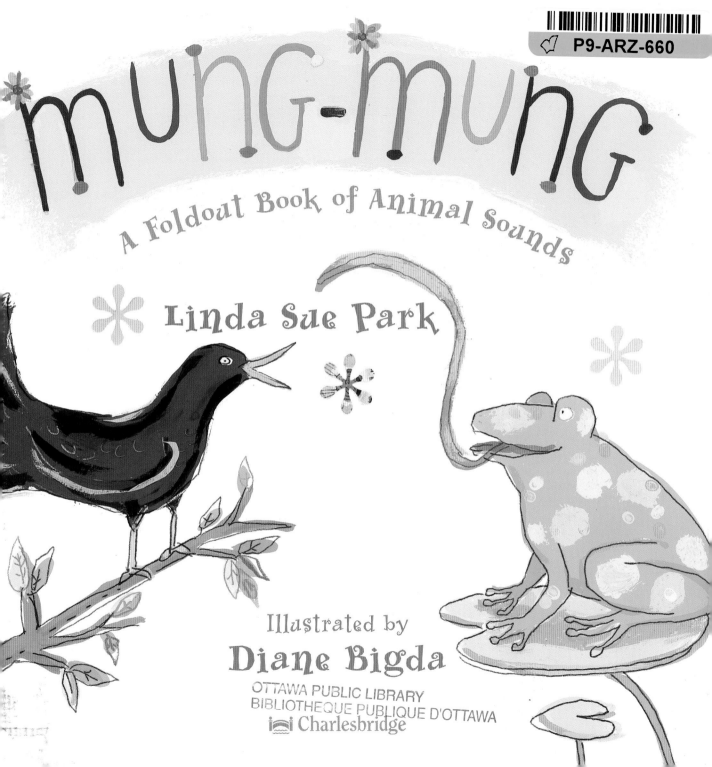

muNG-muNG

A Foldout Book of Animal Sounds

Linda Sue Park

Illustrated by
Diane Bigda

Charlesbridge

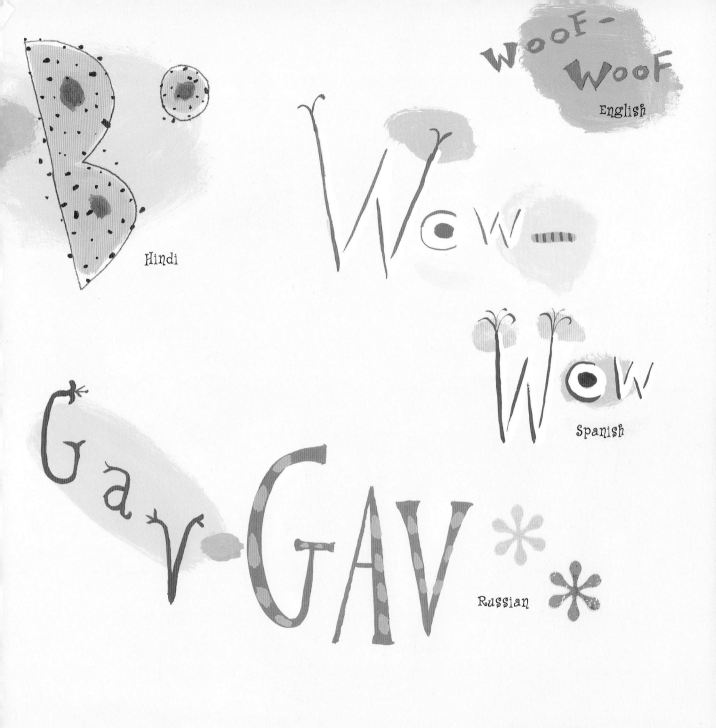

Bo

Hindi

WoW-

Gav·GAV

Wow-
Woof

English

Wow

Spanish

✳
✳

Russian

TWIT

Arabic

JEE · JEE

Chinese

tweet-
tweet.

English

Quee·Quee

French

guo-guo
*
CroA

guo

Chinese

*

RiBBiT-RiBBiT

English

ANIMAL SAYS...

CROA *Spanish*

KO KO KAK *Pilipino*

KaGOL

KaGOL

KaGOL *Korean*

*

What kind of ANIMAL says...

hin-hin
Hindi

EE-HA-HA
Polish

NEIGH
English

VaH

Turkish

*

ga-ga

Japanese

*

Kva-Kva

Swedish

quack

English

WHAT KIND OF

*

Nuff · Nuff

Norwegian

Hoo·Loo

Chinese

ANIMAL SAYS...

oi

oi Vietnamese

* oink

oink English

JWEE

Jwee Spanish

KO · KO

Spanish

Put·Put·Put·Tak

Pilipino

CLUCK-
CLUCK

English

KO·KO DAK·KO

Korean

NGEE-OW

Pilipino

Me-jow

Swedish

EE-OW

Korean

Woof-Woof! Arf-Arf!

If you ask native English speakers what a dog says, you'll get lots of different answers. Ways to make animal sounds vary by country, by region, by dialect, and by family—even within a family!

Bow-Wow!

All the languages in this book are spoken in the
United States as well as in other parts of the world.
The sounds listed are not the only ways to make animal
noises in those languages. Do you know other sounds for
the animals in the book? Can you find out about animal
noises in languages that are not included here?

I am grateful to Dr. Craig Packard of the Center for Applied Linguistics in Washington, D.C., for his assistance in researching this book—L. S. P.

Published by Charlesbridge
85 Main Street
Watertown, MA 02472
(617) 926-0329
www.charlesbridge.com

Library of Congress Cataloging-in-Publication Data
Park, Linda Sue.
  Mang-mang! / Linda Sue Park; illustrated by Diane Bigda.
     p. cm.
  ISBN 1-57091-486-9 (hardcover)
1. Onomatopoeia—Juvenile literature. 2. Animals—Juvenile
literature. I. Bigda, Diane. II. Title.
  P119.P37 2004
  418—dc21   2003003765

Printed in China
(hc) 10 9 8 7 6 5 4 3 2 1

Illustrations done in gouache on Arches paper
Text type set in Whimsy
Color separated, printed, and bound by Jade Productions
Production supervision by Brian G. Walker and Linda Jackson
Designed by Diane Bigda and Susan Mallory Sherman